W9-AAL-957

SEP 1 4

Learning to Read, Step by Step!

Ready to Read   Preschool–Kindergarten
• big type and easy words • rhyme and rhythm • picture clues
For children who know the alphabet and are eager to begin reading.

Reading with Help   Preschool–Grade 1
• basic vocabulary • short sentences • simple stories
For children who recognize familiar words and sound out new words with help.

Reading on Your Own   Grades 1–3
• engaging characters • easy-to-follow plots • popular topics
For children who are ready to read on their own.

Reading Paragraphs   Grades 2–3
• challenging vocabulary • short paragraphs • exciting stories
For newly independent readers who read simple sentences with confidence.

Ready for Chapters   Grades 2–4
• chapters • longer paragraphs • full-color art
For children who want to take the plunge into chapter books but still like colorful pictures.

STEP INTO READING® is designed to give every child a successful reading experience. The grade levels are only guides; children will progress through the steps at their own speed, developing confidence in their reading. The F&P Text Level on the back cover serves as another tool to help you choose the right book for your child.

Remember, a lifetime love of reading starts with a single step!

For Jack and Nate, who helped pull the lever
—S.C.

For my mom and dad,
two great Americans . . . quiet heroes. I love you.
—J.B.

Front cover photograph courtesy of: AP Photo/Carolyn Kaster.
Interior photographs courtesy of: AP Photo/Jae C. Hong, p. 45; AP Photo/Charlie Neibergall,
p. 47; AP Photo/Obama Presidential Campaign, pp. 4, 10; AP Photo/Punahou School, p. 21;
Rex Features via AP Images, p. 48; the White House, p. 5.

This work contains brief excerpts from the following speeches made by Barack Obama: *Wesleyan
University Commencement Address*—May 25, 2008 / Middletown, CT (p. 25); *2004 Democratic
National Convention Keynote Address*—July 27, 2004 / Boston, MA (p. 29); "*A New Era of
Service*" *speech*—July 2, 2008 / Colorado Springs, CO (p. 35); *Election Night Victory Speech*—
November 4, 2008 / Chicago, IL (p. 41); *President Barack Obama's Inaugural Address*—January
20, 2009 / Washington, DC (p. 44); *Election Night Victory Speech*—November 7, 2012 / Chicago, IL
(p. 46).

Visit us on the Web!
StepIntoReading.com
randomhouse.com/kids

Educators and librarians, for a variety of teaching tools, visit us at
RHTeachersLibrarians.com

Library of Congress Cataloging-in-Publication Data
Corey, Shana.
Barack Obama : out of many, one / by Shana Corey ; illustrated by James Bernardin. —
revised ed.
   p. cm.
"A Step 3 book."
ISBN 978-0-375-86339-4 (trade pbk.) — ISBN 978-0-375-97371-0 (lib. bdg.) —
ISBN 978-0-385-37478-1 (ebook)
1. Obama, Barack—Juvenile literature. 2. Presidents—United States—Biography—Juvenile
literature. 3. Racially mixed people—United States—Biography—Juvenile literature.
I. Bernardin, James, ill. II. Title.
E908.C67 2009 973.932092—dc22 [B] 2009007751

Printed in the United States of America
15 14 13 12 11 10 9 8

This book has been officially leveled by using the F&P Text Level Gradient™ Leveling System.

BARACK OBAMA
Out of Many, One

by Shana Corey
illustrated by James Bernardin

Random House New York

We all have stories—
each and every one of us.
This is one of those stories.
It is a story of
a skinny little boy
with a funny name
and how he became part
of America's history.

You've probably heard of him.

His name is Barack Obama.

And he grew up to be

the forty-fourth president of

the United States of America.

Barack Obama was born

in Hawaii

on August 4, 1961.

It was a time when

not everyone believed

black people and white people

should have the same rights.

Barack would help change that.

Barack's mother, Ann, was white.

She was from Kansas.

His father was black.

He was from Kenya.

Barack was named

after his father.

When Barack was two years old,
his father moved far away.
Barack and his mother
lived with his grandpa, Gramps,
and his grandma, Toot.

Barack listened
to his mother's stories
and imagined the father
he did not know.

Hawaii was a wonderful
place for a little boy.
Barack played at the beach.
He ate rice candy and roast pork
and a Hawaiian food called poi.

He went spearfishing with Gramps.
And wherever he went,
he saw many people
of all different colors.

11

In 1967,

Barack's mother remarried.

He and his mother

moved to Indonesia.

It was an adventure!

A pet ape swung in the trees—

right in Barack's backyard.

Two baby crocodiles

swam in a nearby pond.

Barack and his friends

played soccer and caught crickets.

Best of all, Barack had

a new baby sister named Maya.

But there were sad things, too.

When Barack looked in magazines,

he didn't see anyone like him.

No one at school looked like him either.

Barack felt different.

He wondered where he fit in.

And when he looked around,

Barack saw that

many people were sick.

Many people were hungry.

Barack's mother tried to help.

But she could not help everyone.

Barack's mother thought

education was very important.

She brought home books

and speeches for him to read.

Every morning,

she woke him up early to study.

Sometimes he complained.

But his mother made him listen.

She taught him the values

she believed in—

fairness, honesty, and hard work.

Most important,

she taught him that

all people are the same inside.

When he was ten,

Barack won a scholarship

to a school in Hawaii.

He went to live with

Gramps and Toot.

His mother and Maya

joined him the next year.

Barack was smart.
But he wasn't perfect.
Sometimes he was sad.
Sometimes he was angry.
And he still wondered
where he fit in.

That winter,
Barack's father came to visit.
He gave Barack a basketball.
Day after day,
Barack practiced.
Toot always cheered him on.

In high school,

Barack joined

the basketball team.

He liked working

with his teammates

toward a common goal.

At last,

Barack felt like he fit in.

Barack went to college.

He visited museums.

He listened to speeches.

And he spent a lot of time
walking and thinking.

He remembered the poor in Indonesia.

He remembered his mother's lessons
about his own country.

Not that long ago,

people of different colors

could not go to school together.

They could not use

the same water fountains.

Black people could not even vote.

Barack was inspired by

the people who fought to change that.

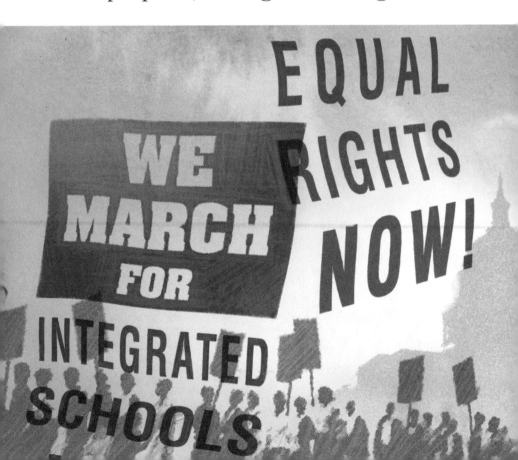

Soon after college,

Barack got a job in Chicago.

He helped people register to vote.

He set up after-school programs

for children.

He worked to get people jobs.

The more he helped others,

the more he understood

his place in the world.

"I discovered how my . . . story

fit into the larger story

of America," he said later.

Barack wanted to fight unfair laws.

So he went to law school.

One summer,

he met a smart young lawyer

named Michelle.

Barack and Michelle got married.

They had two little girls,

Malia and Sasha.

Barack thought the government
could help people have better lives.
So he became a state senator.
Then, in 2004, he ran for the U.S. Senate.
And he won.
That summer, he gave a speech.

He talked about the values
his mother had taught him.
He said that Americans are
one people and we are all equal.
"There is not a black America
and a white America and
a Latino America and an
Asian America—there's the
United States of America!" he said.

Barack's words filled people
with hope.
America was at war.
People needed jobs.
People needed health care.
People listened to Barack
and they believed America
could change.
They believed America
could be better.
People began asking Barack
to run for president!

An African American had never
been elected president.
Many people did not think
Americans would vote
for an African American.
But Barack knew people
were better than that.
On February 10, 2007,
he announced that he was
running for president.

For months and months,

Barack traveled all over America.

He talked about change.

He talked about helping others.

He talked about how together
Americans could make
the world better.
Even kids could help.
"Each of us is free
to seek our own dreams,
but we must also serve
a common purpose," he said.

The more he shared his plans,
the more excited people got.
Pretty soon,
Barack had volunteers
in every state.
They held bake sales
and threw parties.

They put up posters
and handed out flyers.
They went door-to-door
and asked people to vote.

Finally,

it was Election Day!

All over the country,

people came out to vote.

Old people and young people,

people of all colors,

over 130 million people in all.

Many waited in long lines.

Some had mailed in their votes

from far away.

Some had never voted before.

But when they voted,

they all became part

of America's story.

VOTE HE

When the votes were counted,
Barack had won!
Almost 67 million people
had voted for Barack Obama.
That was more votes
than a president
had ever received before!

People danced and cheered and
hugged each other tight.
Many cried tears of joy.
"America is a place
where all things are
possible!" said Obama.

And he was right.
On January 20, 2009,
Barack Obama became
the first African American
president of the United States.
Over a million people
came to Washington, D.C.,
to watch the ceremony.
Millions more saw it on television.

Around the globe,

people of all colors came together

and listened as the new president

spoke of the values his mother

had taught him long ago.

He spoke of working together

and helping others.

"The time has come . . .

to choose our better history!"

he said.

And with that,

a new part of America's story began.

For the next four years, President Obama

worked to make America better.

He worked to end wars.

He worked to make sure all
Americans had health care.

He worked to make sure all
Americans were treated equally.

On November 6, 2012,
Barack Obama was reelected
for a second term.

"I've never been more hopeful
about our future," he said.

"It doesn't matter who you are
or where you come from
or what you look like. . . .
You can make it here in America
if you're willing to try."

But the story is not complete.
In fact, it's just starting.
Where does *your* story
fit in the American story?
You could help your neighbor
or your school.
You could even
grow up to be president!
Anything is possible—
what happens next
is up to you!